FEELING BETTER

Nurturing Self-Esteem

Amy E. Dean

HazeLDeN

First published January, 1988

ISBN 13: 978-089486-486-5

Printed in the United States of America.

PART I

UNDERSTANDING SELF-ESTEEM

*To be nobody but myself — in a world which is
doing its best . . . to make you everybody else — means
to fight the hardest battle which any human being can
fight, and never stop fighting.*
— e e cummings

WHAT IS SELF-ESTEEM?

How we feel about ourselves may be the simplest definition
of self-esteem. The many areas that can influence our self-
assessment include personality, appearance, morality, belief
systems, habits, mannerisms, physical and emotional health,
our feelings of worth, abilities, and capabilities. We may feel
positive about some of those areas and critical of others.

Our feelings about ourselves may change on a daily basis.
One day we may feel strong and in control, self-assured, and
filled with determination. Another day we may feel depressed,
scared, insecure, and unhappy. How do we come to an overall
assessment of how we feel about ourselves if our feelings are in
a constant state of flux?

How we feel about ourselves may be too simplistic a definition for self-esteem, for it doesn't allow for any measurement
or description of our feelings. For the purposes of this pamphlet, self-esteem will be defined as the emotional, physical,
and spiritual value we place upon ourselves.

Our levels of self-esteem may vary in different aspects of
our lives. We may feel confident at work and derive a high
sense of self-esteem in this area. But we may feel unfulfilled in

our intimate relationships and have a low sense of self-esteem in this area.

Understanding Our Sense of Self-esteem

No matter what our sense of self-esteem is today, we weren't born feeling that way. We learned how to feel that way. Much of our learning began in childhood when our parents gave us vital messages about who we were and what our worth was. If we were raised in healthy family environments where we were valued, loved, and nurtured, then chances are we learned to feel good about ourselves because we were shown that others felt good about us.

If we were raised in unhealthy family environments, individuality was discouraged; criticism, abuse, or mixed messages flourished; and nurturing and love were rarely given. Chances are we learned not to feel very good about ourselves because others didn't treat us as if we were very good.

In Part I of this pamphlet, we'll learn more about how the messages we received in childhood have influenced how we feel about ourselves today. We'll discover more about assessing self-esteem and explore how our current levels of self-esteem influence all areas in our lives.

In Part II of this pamphlet, we'll learn how to increase the value of our current levels of self-esteem by using self-esteem building exercises in the following areas.

- *Goal setting*: Setting realistic goals for ourselves.
- *Risk taking*: Learning how to take risks.
- *Opening up*: Establishing relationships with others.
- *Wise choice making*: Choosing what's right for us.
- *Time-sharing*: Using time and patience in our lives.
- *Healing*: Healing our bodies and minds.

The first letters of goal setting, risk taking, opening up, wise choice making, time-sharing, and healing spell GROWTH. These points will be discussed further in Part II.

To begin working on our self-esteem, we first need to take a look at how we arrived at our current feelings about ourselves. The answer may be found by looking back at our childhoods.

ADULT CHILDREN AND SELF-ESTEEM

People who grow up in dysfunctional homes and reach adulthood without dealing with the effects of a nonnurturing childhood are called adult children. The dysfunction in the home could have been exhibited in many ways. These dysfunctions can include active alcohol or other drug addiction, eating disorders, addictive gambling, sexual or physical abuse, mental illness, workaholism, or any other disruption of healthy family interaction that results in a nonnurturing environment. Divorce, separation, and inconsistent guardianship of children by family members or foster homes may also have negative influences on a child's development.

The Influences and Messages of the Past

When dysfunction exists in the home, the focus is usually centered on the dysfunctional parent or parents. The needs of the children are neglected. Without the encouragement, support, and love of a nurturing environment, children in dysfunctional homes can grow to believe certain self-defeating attitudes about who they are. Some of these messages are told to children directly; others are communicated indirectly by the way their parents treat them.

3

We may have interpreted these messages to mean
- We're not important.
- We're in the way.
- We're a problem for ourselves and others.
- We're unattractive.
- We're too loud/too quiet/too _____ (whatever).
- We're not smart; we're stupid.
- We can't do anything right.
- We can't be trusted.
- We're selfish and demanding.
- We'll never amount to anything.
- We aren't loved.
- We aren't wanted or needed.

Assessing Self-esteem

Several components play an important part in determining our levels of self-esteem. How we feel about ourselves in these areas will influence the value we give ourselves. The components include:

- self-acceptance: the feelings we have about ourselves;
- self-worth: the value we place upon ourselves;
- self-feeling: how in touch we are with our feelings;
- self-focus: our ability to look at ourselves;
- self-growth: our commitment to our growth and maturity;
- self-nurturing: our level of caring for ourselves;
- self-guidance: our ability to set a course for our lives;
- self-determination: our commitment to ourselves;

- self-healing: our ability to care for our minds and bodies;
- self-love: our ability to love who we are.

In the following pages we will examine our feelings on these components of self-esteem. After reading the statements that follow each component, we can decide how comfortable we are with the ideas expressed. We may also want to add our own components of self-esteem to the list.

Self-acceptance

I like spending time alone.
I feel happy with the things I do.
I love and appreciate myself for who I am.
I like my appearance.

Self-worth

I believe taking care of myself is important.
I have a lot to give to myself and to others.
I have many good qualities.
I know it's okay to have the things I want.
I am an important person.

Self-feeling

I listen to my feelings and respect them.
I am not afraid of my feelings.
I love to love and to be loved.
I know it's okay to have fun and enjoy myself.

Self-focus

I am the master of my own life.
I do what's right for myself.
I stand up for myself and what I feel.
I am not afraid to be myself.
I know that it's okay to take care of my needs.

Self-growth

I am getting better every day.
I take risks and open up to others.
I accept and make changes in my life.
I feel excited about my growth.
I like setting goals for myself.
I find each day challenging and exciting.

Self-nurturing

I ask for help from others when I need it.
I take good care of myself.
I treat myself the way I'd like others to treat me.
I am patient with myself.
I give love to myself.
I make choices that are right for me.

Self-guidance

I believe I can listen for the guidance offered by a Power
greater than myself.
I know I have strength within me.
I have wisdom and patience to achieve my desires.
I make decisions for myself.

Self-determination

Who I can become is important to me.
I am proud of my accomplishments.
I am always ready to set new goals.
I can do whatever I set out to do.
My life is filled with meaning.

Self-healing

I have a positive attitude.
I treat my body with respect.
I have the power to make myself feel good.
I like how I feel inside.

Self-love

I am not perfect, and this is comfortable.
I attract loving relationships in my life.
I feel happy with my life.
I love myself.

Self-acceptance

When we grow up in dysfunctional homes, we most likely aren't treated as individuals. Dysfunctional parents rarely accept us for who we are. There may be more fault-finding and criticism in our homes than encouragement and praise, no matter how good our efforts are. Therefore, we may grow up with the feeling that we are not acceptable people.

These feelings, when carried into adulthood, can result in our settling for less in life. We may lack the confidence to apply for jobs or try for promotions. We may feel extremely insecure in our relationships. We may avoid any personal challenge because we don't feel we deserve to succeed. When we feel these things, we have a low level of self-acceptance.

If we have an average level of self-acceptance, we may feel fairly comfortable with ourselves most of the time. When we're feeling good about ourselves, we may be willing to take more risks. But when we're feeling not so good, we may tend to be self-critical and more fearful of taking risks. Nevertheless, we believe we are fairly good people and we want to try to achieve success and happiness in our lives.

If we have a high level of self-acceptance, we probably have good feelings about ourselves. We most likely see ourselves as attractive people with good qualities who have a lot to offer. This inner confidence can spill over into all areas of our lives as we seek happiness and challenge on our jobs, in our relationships, and in our personal lives.

The goal of self-acceptance is to feel good about ourselves.

Self-worth

When we grow up in dysfunctional homes, we probably feel we are not valuable or important people. Despite all the recognition and approval we may strive for, our efforts may go unnoticed. Rarely are we given praise or support for our talents and capabilities. Consequently, we may grow up feeling we're not worthwhile people.

This feeling of unworthiness, when carried into adulthood, can result in a belief that we're not important. Much of our lives may seem meaningless, and we may carry an I-don't-care attitude into many facets of our lives. If we don't feel worthwhile, many aspects in our lives may seem worthless. Therefore, we may not invest much time or energy into relationships, careers, and personal growth. When we feel this way about our lives, we have low levels of self-worth.

If we have average levels of self-worth, we may feel we have some value and our lives have some meaning. There may be one or two areas in our lives that are important to us — a job or a relationship, for instance. While we may not feel like a worthwhile person all of the time, we probably do see some personal qualities that are valuable to us and to others in our lives.

If we have a high level of self-worth, we most likely feel a sense of importance to ourselves and of value to others. Our inner feelings of personal worth can help us believe we have a lot to offer. Because of this, success and happiness are usually well within our reach.

The goal of self-worth is to feel like we're valuable, important people.

Self-feeling

When we grow up in dysfunctional homes, acknowledging personal feelings and expressing those feelings are almost always discouraged. Negative feelings such as anger and sadness may be the only emotions exhibited, yet the expression of those feelings may be reserved only for dysfunctional parents. We're usually encouraged to keep our emotions to ourselves or lie about them. Putting on a happy face when we feel miserable inside may keep peace in the house. Therefore, we may grow up believing that what we feel isn't important.

These feelings of unimportance, when carried into adulthood, can result in our being so out of touch with how we feel that we do not show our emotions. Or our range of emotions may be limited to the expression of only one or two feelings, usually the negative feelings prevalent in our childhood homes. When we're out of touch with how to feel and express the wide

9

range of human emotions, we learn not to listen to how we really feel. Growth becomes nearly impossible without understanding our feelings. When we are out of touch with our feelings, we have a low level of self-feeling.

If we have an average level of self-feeling, we may be able to experience some emotions and may even be able to express these emotions. Although we may not know how we feel or know how to express the feelings all of the time, we can usually see improvements in at least one area of our lives — our relationships with others.

If we have high levels of self-feeling, we're probably accepting of our feelings and able to express them when appropriate. We may be able to accept our own positive and negative emotions as well as the emotions of others. As a result, our interactions with others are probably growing and maturing.

The goal of self-feeling is to accept and express our feelings.

Self-focus

When we grow up in dysfunctional homes, we're taught that others are more important. In fact, the focus in the family is usually on the dysfunctional parents. We may not be treated as individuals nor viewed as people who have desires and needs. Therefore, we may grow up with the feeling that others are more important than we are.

When we take these feelings into adulthood, we learn to focus on the needs and wants of others, rather than on our own. We become givers who know no balance between give and take. It may be easy for others to take advantage of our giving natures. As a result, we may feel like victims in our careers or personal relationships because we're unable to stand up for ourselves. When we feel others are more important than we are, we have a low level of self-focus.

If we have average levels of self-focus, we may recognize our needs and desires. We may even be able to communicate those needs and desires to others, but we may be afraid to stand up to some people. But the fact that we're beginning to be in touch with who we are and what we want is the first step toward being able to think of our wants and needs.

If we have high levels of self-focus, we are most likely able to stand up for ourselves and how we feel. We're probably able to make decisions based on what's right for us, and we can think of ourselves without being selfish.

The goal of self-focus is to be the master of our lives.

Self-growth

When we grow up in dysfunctional homes, our maturing and growing process is usually ignored because we're not seen as individuals with personal sets of needs. Because of this, rarely are we encouraged to take risks or make changes in our lives that will help us grow as individuals. Therefore, we may grow up with the feeling that we're stuck being the people we are, whether we like it or not.

When we feel stunted in our growth as adults, we may find we don't know how to help ourselves grow. We don't know how to take risks, make changes, or walk away from stagnating relationships or dead-end jobs. When we feel stunted, we have a low level of self-growth.

If we have an average level of self-growth, chances are we can take some risks and make some changes in our lives. Although these risks and changes may be quite simple, the fact that we're ready to make them shows an acceptance of the need to help ourselves grow.

If we have a high level of self-growth, we may see each day as another chance for personal growth. We may be able to ask for help from others because we look upon the help we get as part of the positive steps we're making in our growth. The risks we take may be so significant that we may find it difficult to keep up with the momentum of our decisions. But overall, we probably feel a sense of personal satisfaction and reward.

The goal of self-growth is to become healthier and happier.

Self-nurturing

When we grow up in dysfunctional homes, rarely are we given encouragement, support, and love — the three components of nurturing. We may be ignored, abused, or mistreated or given confusing, mixed messages about the feelings our parents have for us. Therefore, we may grow up without any idea of what nurturing is all about.

When we lack nurturance, rarely can we give encouragement, support, and love to ourselves. Because of this, we may have a difficult time learning who we are, how we feel, what path in life is right for us, and which people can help our growth. Therefore, we have a low level of self-nurturing.

If we have average levels of self-nurturing, we're most likely able to make some choices that are right for us, although we might not always know what we'd like or how we feel. We may take good care of ourselves most of the time. We may have some idea of how to nurture ourselves, but may not be able to do it on a consistent basis.

If we have high levels of self-nurturing, we are most likely able to encourage, support, and love ourselves on a consistent basis. Because of this, we're probably able to make decisions that are right for us. We take risks and give ourselves time and room to grow.

The goal of self-nurturing is to give lovingly to ourselves.

Self-guidance

When we grow up in dysfunctional homes, there's usually no one there to guide our growth. We may feel inadequate when it comes to learning how to care for ourselves. Consequently, we may grow up with few skills to chart the course of our lives and growth.

When we are without guidance, we're like a ship floundering on stormy seas. With no steering mechanism, we may have no idea how to depend on ourselves for inner strength and guidance. Therefore, we have a low level of self-guidance.

If we have average levels of self-guidance, we may have some inkling that our ability to grow and mature lies within us. Sometimes we may listen to our inner guide, but may not rely on it. Some days we may feel strong and sure of ourselves; other days we may feel directionless and insecure with our judgment.

If we have high levels of self-guidance, we most likely believe in our own inner strengths and have faith in a power outside of ourselves to help us build strength. Therefore, we are able to use this faith to set realistic goals for ourselves and to trust that all the happiness and success we'd like to achieve can be ours, with time and patience.

The goal of self-guidance is to trust our ability to guide ourselves.

Self-determination

When we grow up in dysfunctional homes, rarely do we learn how to stick with goals in a healthy way. Our childhood homes may be filled with the chaos of unfinished projects or organized to the point of obsession. Rarely is there balance. In addition, we may watch our dysfunctional parents try repeatedly and unsuccessfully to kick their addictions or make changes in their lives. Therefore, we may grow up with the feeling that it's not important to excel or to try our best in anything.

When we grow up without understanding the importance of setting and reaching goals, we may give up easily. We learn to see molehills as mountains and achievements as unattainable. Therefore, we may rarely set goals for ourselves, avoid taking any risks, and drift aimlessly from job to job or relationship to relationship, not putting much effort into making anything work. We have a low level of self-determination.

If we have average levels of self-determination, we may set some goals for ourselves and, if they're realistic, may achieve them. But the effort we put into their attainment may be sporadic, depending on the strength of our determination. If a job or a person means a great deal to us, we may work hard at achieving career success or at working out relationship difficulties.

If we have high levels of self-determination, our accomplishments are most likely a source of pride for us. Therefore, we are usually ready to set new goals, take risks, and achieve our aspirations.

The goal of self-determination is to feel that who we can become is vital.

Self-healing

When we grow up in dysfunctional homes, we grow up in environments that can be unhealthy in three ways: physically, emotionally, and spiritually. Therefore, we may grow up unable to recognize how to feel better on the inside or outside.

When we carry this empty feeling into adulthood, we're left virtually unprotected from the effects that negative messages and behaviors can have on the mind and body. We may be physically sick or prone to accidents a great deal of the time. We may be depressed or lethargic. And, even though we may dislike feeling the way we do, we may not know how to help ourselves feel better except by medication, or isolation, or both. Therefore, we have a low level of self-healing.

If we have average levels of self-healing, we may be able to make some changes in our health. For example, we may start eating healthier food or start exercising to improve our appearance and physical strength. Nevertheless, we may not recognize the importance our mental and spiritual well-being has upon our health. Therefore, while we may feel pleased with the outer changes we're making, we may still feel unhealthy or unhappy and not know how to make inner changes.

If we have high levels of self-healing, we probably know the mental, physical, and spiritual parts of ourselves are connected to overall health. We may be working on changes and improvements in all three areas.

The goal of self-healing is to feel good about ourselves, inside and out.

Self-love

When we grow up in dysfunctional homes, rarely are we shown what love really is. Often love is shown in negative ways, by abuse, abandonment, and rejection. Because we grow up with such negative feelings of what love is, we don't learn how to give ourselves positive love, and we don't know how to accept positive love. Therefore, we may grow up with the feeling that negative love is all we deserve.

When we carry unloving feelings into adulthood, we may perpetuate the forms of love we've been shown. We don't learn how to give or receive positive love. Therefore, we may have great difficulty forming relationships and may treat ourselves in negative ways. When we feel unloving, we have a low level of self-love.

If we have average levels of self-love, we feel that we like ourselves more than we love ourselves. We may feel happy with ourselves from time to time and may form meaningful relationships held together by positive bonds.

If we have a high level of self-love, we probably can say that we love ourselves. We most likely feel happy with our lives, who we are, and where we're going. We may feel happy just being alive and waking up to the challenge and excitement of each new day.

The goal of self-love is to be able to love ourselves.

How we can reach the goals for each component of self-esteem and improve our overall sense of self-esteem will be explored in Part II.

PART II

BUILDING SELF-ESTEEM

Change your thoughts, and you change your world.
— the Reverend Norman Vincent Peale

The key word in this section is *change*. In order to improve our sense of self-esteem, we need to begin to change. It has been said that if we don't choose to act differently we will simply behave in ways that are familiar to us. But changes can mean new behaviors; new behaviors can mean new experiences; new experiences can mean healthy growth.

To effect positive changes in our levels of self-esteem, we need to remember one word: GROWTH. That word can be seen as an acronym for the six specific areas of self-esteem that were mentioned in Part I: goal setting, risk taking, opening up, wise choice making, time-sharing, and healing.

Working through an understanding of these six areas and using exercises to initiate positive changes in our levels of self-esteem are the goals for Part II.

Goal Setting

One component to building our level of self-esteem is goal setting. If we don't have anything to work toward in our daily lives, we may find it difficult to feel motivated, challenged, and excited. If we're not achieving ideals set for ourselves, then we may find it difficult to feel good about ourselves. If we don't have something to set our sights on, we may never know what we're capable of attaining.

But when we set goals and work toward reaching them, we learn about our capabilities, needs, wants, and desires.

How to Set Goals for Ourselves

To begin setting goals we need to make our goals realistic. There's no better way to feed an already low level of self-esteem than to set an unreasonable goal.

> EXAMPLE: If we hold an entry-level position at work, we shouldn't say we want to be managers within a year. To make our goals more realistic, we can decide we want to have at least one promotion this year. That way, we set our sights one step above our present positions, not several steps.

We can also remember to set goals that are appropriate for us. We should be true to ourselves, not to someone we think we should be.

> EXAMPLE: We want to get ourselves in better physical shape. We see a picture of a marathon runner and decide that's what we want to look like. Even though we hate to run, we set goals to compete in marathons. Each day we run is a chore. We finally give up and hate ourselves for not achieving what we set out to do. To make our goal more realistic, we can decide what forms of exercise we like to do or would like to learn. Then we set more attainable goals and try that form of exercise.

In goal setting, we can consider the importance of building assessment periods into our goals. This will allow us time to look at our goals and determine whether they're still appropriate or not. Without time constraints on our goals, we may find ourselves with no escapes or built-in change factors. When we're stuck with endless goals, the only alternatives are for us

to stick with situations that may be unbearable, or give up —
neither of which is good for our self-esteem.

   EXAMPLE: After we determine the exercises we'd
   like to try, we set time limits on them; say, two weeks.
   At the end of the two-week period, we decide how
   we feel about the exercise programs and revise them,
   if necessary. We may end up trying a few programs
   over a couple of months before we finally end up with
   something we really enjoy and want to stick with.

   Effective goal setting is to set goals in all areas of our
lives. Many people think they should only have goals for areas
outside of themselves, like careers, schooling, or travel. But
goal setting can help support our sense of self-esteem in all
areas: interactions with others, family lives, hobbies, personal
achievements, and intimate relationships.

   EXAMPLE: We don't like how we communicate
   with others. We can set goals of learning how to
   improve our communication skills and set time constraints of two weeks in which to reassess improvements made or changes needed.

   In setting goals it's good to know how to achieve our goals
before or as we set them, or to know who to ask for help in
achieving them. Unless we have some guidelines on how to
reach our goals, our goals will most likely remain unattainable.

   EXAMPLE: If we have no idea how to improve
   our communication skills, our communications with
   others will probably not get better. But if our friends
   give us specific advice such as, ''I don't like it when

19

you jump to conclusions before I explain myself,"
then we can work on listening before we leap.

Setting goals means we have to be willing to take risks.

Risk Taking

If we don't learn how to open up to others, it will be hard
for us to improve our interactions with others and increase our
levels of intimacy. If we don't accept certain challenges that
come our way, we may never discover our abilities. If we don't
risk being vulnerable, we won't be able to grow. If we don't
try to reach for the stars every once in a while, we'll forever be
admiring them from afar!

But when we take risks, we open ourselves up to the
possibilities of becoming who we'd like to be. Through risk
taking, limitations and fears can be worked through.

How to Risk Taking Risks

Our risks should be worthwhile. We should set realistic goals and use risk taking to help attain those goals. We
shouldn't take risks to prove we can take risks, but for the
challenges and growth they can give to our self-esteem.

EXAMPLE: We may believe skydiving to be the
ultimate in risks. But there's no point in undertaking
it if it won't help us build our self-esteem.

In taking risks, we should do things that are appropriate
for us and our growth in particular areas. Think about what
types of risks we can take that can help us, not hinder us.

EXAMPLE: We want to feel more confident in
ourselves and what we can do. In that case, skydiving

may be a risktaking choice that can help build our confidence. But if we have a fear of heights and hate feeling out of control, we may be better off taking a risk that's more suited to our personalities.

Risks shouldn't be taken for the praise we may get from others, but for the pride we'll feel in ourselves and the fulfillment we can gain. We shouldn't focus on how others may view what we do, but focus on ourselves. Otherwise, we'll be dependent on what others think rather than what we think.

EXAMPLE: Our friends have pointed out our shyness in social situations. We know they're right, and we'd like to feel more self-confident. When we receive an invitation to attend a company outing, we decide to go even though we don't particularly like our co-workers. We accept only to impress our friends and earn their approval for what we did, which won't build our self-esteem.

To take a risk is to give ourselves credit for what we try, even if we fail. Our self-esteem shouldn't rest on the outcome of risk taking; it should rest on the effort it took to affect the outcome.

EXAMPLE: We attend the company outing because we want to work on overcoming our shyness. Yet we end up sitting in the corner the entire time, not talking to anyone. We still need to give ourselves credit for taking the risk and attending the social event. Just because the outing didn't work out the way we wanted doesn't mean we didn't succeed. We actually did achieve what we set out to do because we took the risk and attended the outing.

21

One purpose of risk taking is to open up to others.

Opening Up

If we don't let others see us for who we really are, it may be hard for us to take risks. If we don't share our inner feelings, both good and bad, it may be easy for us to deny or disguise how we really feel. If we don't let others see our human qualities — our successes as well as our failures — it may be difficult for us to strive for anything less than perfection. If we don't reveal ourselves to others, it may be difficult to learn how to trust.

When we let others see us for who we really are, it can become easier for us to see ourselves too.

How to Open Up to Others

We need to accept ourselves for who we are. Unless we're honest first with ourselves, it may be difficult to be honest with others. Without honesty, we run the risk of denying our feelings, becoming out of touch with how we really think or feel, forfeiting closeness and caring from others, and sacrificing self-nurturing.

> EXAMPLE: A friend invites us to a potluck dinner. We have food allergies that cause us physical discomfort when they're ignored. But because we hate having the allergies and calling any special attention to our needs, we decide not to share that we can only eat certain foods. We go to the dinner, eat the foods, and become ill.

We must prepare ourselves to accept the feelings and maybe the criticisms of others. Just as we may find it difficult

to accept who we really are, others may have the same difficulty. Some may criticize us or pass judgment on our beliefs,
behaviors, or personality traits. To build our self-esteem, we
need to keep in mind that we have the power to accept or
reject the thoughts of others. What's most important is what
we think about who we are and what we do.

EXAMPLE: We're the shy person who took a risk
and attended the company outing. When we proudly
tell a friend what we did and she asks if we talked with
anybody, she may become critical when she hears we
sat in a corner the whole time. It's okay that she feels
the way she does. But we shouldn't let her comments
or criticism take away the pride we have in our risk
taking efforts.

One purpose of opening up is to learn about ourselves as
we risk opening up to others. As we become more visible to
others, we try to see ourselves more clearly.

EXAMPLE: We can use a journal to record our
risk taking experiences. We can write about how
we felt, what others said to us when we shared our
experiences, and how we felt about what they said.
We should try to be as objective as possible in order to
gain the most from this.

In opening up to others, we need to learn when and who
to trust. It's not a good idea to open up to everyone. We
need to learn which people we can trust to give us support and
encouragement as we share.

EXAMPLE: We've had another argument with our
parents and really need to talk to someone about our

feelings. We decide to share how we feel with people we've dated a few times. We may find ourselves more frustrated and upset because these people know very little about us and can't really be supportive.

The process of opening up is making wise choices.

Wise Choice Making

If we don't know how to make decisions that are right for us, we may end up frustrated. Knowing who to trust and when to trust is part of wise choice making. Knowing how to focus on ourselves and make decisions based on what's right for us is also a part of wise choice making. When we know how to make the right choices, we can then become more self-confident and self-nurturing.

How to Make Wise Choices

In order to make choices, we need to listen to ourselves. How do we feel? What do we want? What's right for us? What's wrong for us? Unless we can listen to ourselves and answer questions like these when it is time to make decisions, we may be incapable of making personally satisfying decisions.

> EXAMPLE: It's Friday night. We have the choice of seeing a friend, shopping for our sister's birthday present, running some errands, or staying home and reading a book. Unless we can make a choice between what we want to do and what we need to do, we may have a difficult time choosing anything.

The choice involved in deciding what we *want* to do and what we *need* to do can sometimes be solved by taking a look at where our life needs balance.

EXAMPLE: We may have had an extremely difficult work week and find the last thing we want to do on our Friday night is run errands or shop for a birthday present. Since the scales have been tipped in the direction of responsibility for most of the week, we can balance the scales by socializing with our friends or spending the time alone.

To make wise choices, we need to use our time effectively.

Time-Sharing

Time, in this case, also includes patience. We need both time and patience with ourselves and our growth to develop high levels of self-esteem. If we push ourselves too quickly, we may find ourselves stepping backward instead of forward. If we don't allow ourselves room to grow, we may find ourselves doing more stagnating than renewing. When we use time and patience effectively in our lives, we let the passage of time work for us, not against us.

How to Use Time-Sharing

Effective time-sharing means making changes at our own pace. Our rates of growth are going to be different than the rates for others. We need to learn how to grow within a time frame that fits our needs and personalities.

EXAMPLE: A co-worker who joined the company at the same time and in the same position as we did has been promoted twice in the past year. Our goal was originally to be promoted one step above our current position within a year. But now we revise our goal to match our co-worker's promotion. When we finally are promoted once within the year, we're disappointed rather than elated.

In learning effective time-sharing, it's a good idea to use our journals and any other records of our lives to assess our growth after a period of time, not on a daily basis. Growth is best seen when reviewed after a few months, six months, or even a year.

Finally, effective time-sharing means using healing to help our growth.

Healing

Healing includes our physical health and well-being, involving the interaction between our minds and bodies. Healing is threefold: mind, body, and spirit. If we're not feeling emotionally well, our bodies will most likely suffer. If our bodies are out of shape, our emotional outlooks may be negatively affected. If we don't have faith in our connections to everything around us, then we will probably lack the determination necessary to feel well and think clearly.

When we learn how to heal our minds and bodies, we're in a much better position to ease some of the self-defeating characteristics that have affected our levels of self-esteem.

How to Use Healing

To heal effectively we must see ourselves as good people. The best way to do this is to take time each day for one or two weeks to list at least five qualities that we like about ourselves — without repeating a quality from one day to the next. With this exercise, we're forced to look deep inside ourselves as we think of five different qualities each day.

Some of us may need to take better care of our appearance. This can include better grooming, paying more attention